Caught & Told

SANDEEP PATIL, born in 1956, was one of the most entertaining players on the international stage in the 1980s. In his five-year-long international career he came up with some sterling performances. In Australia in 1980-81 he took on the likes of Dennis Lillee, Len Pascoe and Rodney Hogg to plunder 174 at the Adelaide Oval. If that was his finest hour, he gave power hitting a good name when he scored 24 off Bob Willis in a single over at Old Trafford in 1982.

When not wielding his willow, Patil had other interests and these included editing a Marathi magazine called *Shatkar*. He is a known prankster and is never short of a story, some of which have made it to this collection of anecdotes.

CLAYTON MURZELLO once sold sports books at Marine Sports, the only specialist sports bookshop in India, before deciding to get closer to his favourite sport, cricket. He leapt into journalism in 1989 and today is Sports Editor of *Mid-Day*, India's largest-selling tabloid. Murzello has covered cricket in five countries, and been to two World Cups. At the 2005 Sports Journalists Federation of India awards, Murzello won the prize for the best offbeat story.

OTHER LOTUS TITLES:

Aitzaz Ahsan	*The Indus Saga: The Making of Pakistan*
Alam Srinivas	*Storms in the Sea Wind: Ambani vs Ambani*
Amir Mir	*The True Face of Jehadis: Inside Pakistan's Terror Networks*
Bidyut Chakrabarty	*Gandhi: A Historical Biography*
Chaman Nahal	*Silent Life: Memoirs of a Writer*
Duff Hart-Davis	*Honorary Tiger: The Life of Billy Arjan Singh*
Frank Simoes	*Frank Unedited*
Frank Simoes	*Frank Simoes' Goa*
M.G. Devasatayam	*JP in Jail: An Uncensored Account*
M.J. Akbar	*India: The Siege Within*
M.J. Akbar	*Kashmir: Behind the Vale*
M.J. Akbar	*Nehru: The Making of India*
M.J. Akbar	*Riot after Riot*
M.J. Akbar	*The Shade of Swords*
M.J. Akbar	*Byline*
M.J. Akbar	*Blood Brothers: A Family Saga*
Meghnad Desai	*Nehru's Hero Dilip Kumar: In the Life of India*
Nayantara Sahgal (ed.)	*Before Freedom: Nehru's Letters to His Sister*
Neesha Mirchandani	*Wisdom Song: The Life of Baba Amte*
Rohan Gunaratna	*Inside Al Qaeda*
Maj. Gen. (Retd) Ian Cardozo	*Param Vir: Our Heroes in Battle*
Maj. Gen. (Retd) Ian Cardozo	*The Sinking of INS Khukri: Survivors' Stories*
Maj. R.P. Singh, Kanwar Rajpal Singh	*Sawai Man Singh II of Jaipur: Life and Legend*
Mushirul Hasan	*India Partitioned. 2 Vols*
Mushirul Hasan	*John Company to the Republic*
Rachel Dwyer	*Yash Chopra: Fifty Years of Indian Cinema*
Satish Jacob	*From Hotel Palestine Baghdad*
Shrabani Basu	*Spy Princess: The Life of Noor Inayat Khan*
Thomas Weber	*Gandhi, Gandhism and the Gandhians*
Vaibhav Purandare	*Sachin Tendulkar: A Difinitive Biography*
Verghese Kurien, as told to Gouri Salvi	*I Too Had a Dream*

FORTHCOMING TITLES:

Bidyut Chakrabarty	*Gandhi: A Historical Biography*
Bhavana Somaya	*Hema Malini: The Authorised Biography*
Leela Kirloskar	*The Essential Handbook of Divorce*
BK Trehan, Indu Trehan	*The Joys of Retirement*

Caught & Told

Humorous Cricketing Anecdotes

Sandeep Patil
Clayton Murzello

Illustrations
Austin Coutinho

LOTUS COLLECTION
ROLI BOOKS

Lotus Collection

© PRO Sports & Jai Bokey 2007
All rights reserved. No part of this publication may be
reproduced or transmitted, in any form or by any means,
without the prior permission of the publisher.

First published in India by Roli Books in 2007

The Lotus Collection
An imprint of
Roli Books Pvt. Ltd.
M-75, G.K. II Market
New Delhi 110 048
Phones: ++91 (011) 2921 2271, 2921 2782
2921 0886, Fax: ++91 (011) 2921 7185
E-mail: roli@vsnl.com; Website: rolibooks.com
Also at
Bangalore, Varanasi, Mumbai and Jaipur

Book concept: Jai Bokey
Design: Kumar Raman
Production: Kumar Raman & Naresh Nigam

ISBN: 81-7436-496-X
Rs 195/-

Typeset in Frutiger 47 light cn by Roli Books Pvt. Ltd. and
printed at Anubha Printers, Noida.

Acknowledgements

CRICKETERS: Kiran Ashar, Ian Chappell, Rahul Dravid, Raj Singh Dungarpur, Anshuman Gaekwad, Sourav Ganguly, Karsan Ghavri, Sanjay Jagdale, Vinod Kambli, Raju Kulkarni, Bharat Kunderan, Arun Lal, Ashley Mallett, Ashok Mankad, Kiran More, Ashish Nehra, Chandrakant Pandit, Vasu Paranjape, Milind Rege, Balwinder Singh Sandhu, Virender Sehwag, T.A. Sekhar, Yajurvindra Singh, Javagal Srinath, Sachin Tendulkar, Glenn Turner, Ajit Wadekar and John Wright.

JOURNALISTS: Qamar Ahmad, Khalid A.H. Ansari, Harpal Singh Bedi, Raju Bharatan, Rahul Bhattacharya, Gulu Ezekiel, Nagaraj Gollapudi, Ramachandra Guha, Gideon Haigh, Kuldip Lal, Kersi Meher-Homji, H. Natrajan, Aakar Patel, Mudar Patherya, G. Rajaraman, S.S. Ramaswamy, Sharda Ugra, Anand Vasu, Pradeep Vijayakar and Makarand Waingankar.

OTHER CONTRIBUTORS: Tom Alter, Hemant Kenkre and Devendra Prabhudesai.

Foreword

The great thing about cricket is that it produces so many characters and so many funny moments. One reason for this is the sheer length of the game.

Our shorter version of the game is twice as long as any other sport. So, there is a lot of time for things to happen and develop. Some of the game's great characters use their time productively playing practical jokes on their mates. The sort of creative mind that you need to be successful at cricket is very useful for practical jokes.

Most of the players I played with, those who survived any length of time, did stay because they had a good sense of humour. They could laugh at themselves, at others and at serious moments as much as funny ones. You need characters in a cricket team. There are plenty of times when you could take yourself too seriously.

To have someone like Doug Walters in the dressing room or out on the field just to lighten those serious moments was a good way to be able to survive. I am sure one of the reasons why we (Australia) became a good side was because we had a lot of characters.

You will find that most good teams have such characters. They are not all the same though. Some are funny because they are serious and their teammates take the mickey out of them because they are so serious. I have seen guys get over their seriousness and begin to see the lighter side of life. It helped them become better cricketers.

Whilst cricket has become more of a game of statistics these days, it has really been more of a game of stories. There are probably more books written on cricket than on other sports and I am sure it is because of the duration of the game, which allows many funny moments.

In days gone by, after the day's play, we talked cricket and told stories. I think the folklore of the game has survived and the game is richer because of its characters and stories.

I am sure readers of the book will enjoy the stories in these pages.

– Greg Chappell

Paaji's Pants Peeve

After a lunch break one day during the 1992-93 Durban Test against South Africa, I walked on to the field feeling nicely pumped up to do battle against the feisty South Africans. As soon as I reached my fielding position, I could hear Kapil Dev calling out to me from the dressing room. What is he still doing in the dressing room, I thought. I soon discovered that he was admonishing me for wearing his trousers. In all the excitement of the Test, I had put on his pair, which was kept for drying in the dressing room. I had never seen Paaji so furious before.

— Javagal Srinath

Vish I Knew

In the 1974-75 Test series against Clive Lloyd's West Indians, paceman Vanburn Holder bowled Gundappa Vishwanath during the dying moments of the day's play in the second innings of the last Test at the Wankhede Stadium. After the game, a TV commentator asked Vishy whether the ball was an inswinger or outswinger. Vishy replied nonchalantly: 'If I'd known that, I would still be batting.'

— Hemant Kenkre

Zail Terms

Soon after the historic World Cup victory in 1983, President Zail Singh hosted a tea party for the Indian team in the plush lawns of the Rashtrapati Bhavan in New Delhi. The president asked Kapil Dev, who had captained India to the famous win, as to what the team planned to do. Kapil replied that they would be going to the States (meaning the US). The president misunderstood and gave a nod of approval: 'Of course, of course, you should go to all the states – Gujarat, Maharashtra, Uttar Pradesh, Punjab,...' Kapil could only agree to that.

– Sandeep Patil

Baby of the Team

On a flight during Sachin Tendulkar's early days as an Indian Test player, Sunil Gavaskar informed the air hostess that there was a baby on the flight and asked her to provide him a glass of milk. The glass of milk promptly made it to the back rows. And Tendulkar drank it!

– Sandeep Patil

Nick Pick

The horror stories I had heard about Indian umpires before our 1969 tour came to a naught after an incident that more than proved how smart they were. During our game against North Zone, Johnny Gleeson's unorthodox spin had the Indian batsmen groping, pushing and prodding, shuffling and swishing. But not once could they connect bat to ball. When one of them finally did, he had edged one to the wicketkeeper, Brian Taber. The loud appeal, however, had no effect on the umpire, who would have shamed a rock with his 'standing still' ability. The bowler, the wicketkeeper and the close-in fielders were dumbstruck, until a player from cover appealed again, after which the umpire's finger went up. As we gathered in a group to congratulate Gleeson and Taber, the umpire walked the length of the pitch, tapped Johnny on the shoulder, and said, 'Mr Gleeson, I am sorry to have taken so long over that decision, but there was a strong wind blowing against me and it took a long time for the sound of the nick to carry to my end.'

– Ian Chappell

Duck Cluck

Back in Mumbai from a disastrous tour of Australia on the batting front, an Indian all-rounder, who had scored more ducks than even his opponents had bargained for, thought it was a good idea to get back to the nets, despite a niggle he suffered from. A former India player decided to drop in too. Suddenly the younger man was seen limping and was promptly asked as to what was wrong. 'I'd slipped while taking the second run on the tour,' came the response. The old pro saw the irony. 'Second run? When did you get the first run,' he asked.

– Clayton Murzello

Worry Flurry

Vasu Paranjape, who knows a bit of palmistry, was amazed to see Krishnamachari Srikkanth's palm. Srikkanth said: 'Look, I have no lines on my palms, so I have no worries.' Vasu replied: 'You are right; there are no worries for you. All the worries are for those who watch you bat.'

– Sandeep Patil

Die Ha(rd)!

I was sent to Australia as a replacement for Surinder Amarnath in 1977-78, my first tour to that country. The day I arrived, our captain Bishen Bedi took me to the Australian dressing room at the Melbourne Cricket Ground. 'Have you come here to die,' one of the officials asked me. I was taken aback and gave him a firm 'No'. I was asked again. Again, I said 'No'. Bishen overheard the conversation and intervened. 'Charlie, you are not understanding his question. He is asking if you have come here *today*?' My first test with the Australian accent had just ended disastrously.

– Anshuman Gaekwad

True Good

On the 1990 tour to England, Sunil Gavaskar asked former England fast bowler Freddie Trueman whether he remembered his uncle Madhav Mantri, who had played against Trueman in the 1952 series in England, and was now the manager of the present team. In his inimitable style, Trueman replied that he did not recollect Mantri because none of the Indians stayed at the crease too long when he was bowling! Right said Fred.

– Sandeep Patil

Hair Fare

In the early '80s, Sandeep Patil had a huge fan following. It was largely because of his big hitting and the casual ease with which he dispatched bowlers like Dennis Lillee and Bob Willis to the boundary. He was somewhat of an enigma though, for he had the knack of getting himself injured at the most inopportune moments. Our team doctor those days – Vishwas Raut – was a university-level cricketer himself. Whenever Sandeep came down with an injury, he gave the media only one reason for it: 'Hairline fracture.' I was fed up with this standard answer, so I told Sandeep to take a close look at the X-ray machine the next time he visited Dr Raut's clinic. 'Why,' he asked. 'Because I am pretty sure you will see a hair on its screen,' I replied.

– Balwinder Singh Sandhu

Cricket Talk

My habit of sleepwalking has given others a lot of sleepless nights, but nothing more than my habit of talking while in my sleep. As my roommate during my debut tour of Pakistan in 1989, Kiran More heard me shout more than once in my sleep: 'Maro, maro... that's a four.' But what shocked him more was that during one of these spells, I even broke my *kada* (bracelet).

– Sachin Tendulkar

Arjun Run-outunga!

In my debut Test against Sri Lanka at the Sinhalese Sports Club in Colombo in 1999, I was fielding on the boundary line when a problem with the sightscreen caught my attention. Since play was halted, I thought it was a good time to sit down and tie my laces. Suddenly, I noticed that a new player was walking out to bat and I wondered when in the world that had happened. I soon realised that I had totally missed my teammates' appeal for a run-out decision against Arjuna Ranatunga, who had been declared out by the third umpire. The sightscreen problem just happened in the process.

– Ashish Nehra

Operation Flood

At the national under-15 camp in Indore, there were no greater bullies than Sachin Tendulkar and Vinod Kambli. We were staying at the Nehru Stadium premises when suddenly one evening my roomie and I woke up to the sight of water flooding my room. The rest of the afternoon went in salvaging our equipment. Even as we were wondering about the source of the water, I saw a pipe below our room door. Messrs Tendulkar and Kambli were at it again. A small argument between us in the morning had provoked this act of vengeance. And 'water' revenge it was! Our coach Vasu Paranjape ensured that we never fought with each other again on the tour.

– Sourav Ganguly

Run Riot

Harbhajan Singh was not in the Indian team when I took over as coach for the home series against Zimbabwe. I first met Bhajji when the Indian team gathered in Chennai for a camp to prepare for the historic series against Australia in 2001. I asked him to run a few laps of the ground, and then had to rush into the pavilion to take a call from the Board of Control for Cricket in India. When I returned to the nets, I started looking for Bhajji and was told that he was still running. That was nearly ninety minutes after I got that telephone call! I felt embarrassed, but Bhajji was obedient as ever.

– John Wright

As a Manure of Fact...

While Dilip Vengsarkar was supervising the setting up of his academy amidst piles of mud and clay, a member of the Mumbai cricket fraternity decided to take a look at the work in progress. Vengsarkar was bemused to see this person urinating on the soil. When asked what was he up to, the visitor reasoned that his urine would act as perfect manure.

– Makarand Waingankar

Slip and a 'Gaali'

My fellow national selector Madan Lal once landed in Guwahati (Assam) for a one-day game. Normally, local organisers send someone to receive a selector. So, naturally, Madan expected someone to be waiting for him at the airport, as he did not know the city well. He looked around, but there was no one. After a while, when his patience ran out, he took out the Board of Control for Cricket in India telephone directory, and dialled the first number listed under Assam Cricket Association. Once connected, he dished out the choicest expletives. The person on the other side apologised profusely, and Madan somehow managed to reach his hotel.

The next day, Madan met the secretary of the association and admonished him for not picking him up from the airport on time. The secretary was apologetic, and then asked Madan how he managed to get to his hotel. When Madan told him about how the phone call did the trick, the secretary had a strange look on his face.

The reason? Madan had called up Assam's chief minister Prafulla Kumar Mahanta. Since Mahanta was also the president of the Assam Cricket Association, his number was on top of the page in the directory. Madan was so embarrassed he was seen avoiding the chief minister whenever the latter would make his way to the selectors' box.

– Sanjay Jagdale

Sunny Funny

When India toured Australia in 1980-81, they played a warm-up game in Perth, where the West Australian Cricket Association (WACA) held a luncheon in their honour. The master of ceremonies was called upon to introduce the captain of the visiting team. He said, 'I would now like to welcome a man small of stature but a giant among cricketers. India's greatest batsman, perhaps the best player in the world at the present time, currently second only to Sir Donald Bradman on the all-time list of century-makers (as he was then).

'Ladies and gentlemen, could you please put your hands together for "Sir Neil Gavaskar!"'

– Gideon Haigh

Coach Hunte

They say success has many fathers. This story is a perfect example. Conrad Hunte, the former West Indian batsman, was among the overseas players who attended Sunil Gavaskar's wedding reception. The affable Hunte took a while before he got on stage to greet the couple. And when he made it, he exclaimed to Gavaskar: 'Now I know why you are such a good player. It is because you have so many coaches. I met twenty of them on the way up here.'

– Makarand Waingankar

Hutton Chops

At the inaugural 1975 Prudential World Cup, all participating teams were invited for cocktails at Lord's. With wine glasses in hand, Karsan Ghavri and I were at the window of the famous Long Room. This was our first big outing with the team; we were, naturally, nervous. As we were talking, an old man approached us and began asking questions. We thought he was an old cranky MCC member, so we did not really bother to answer. We tried several tactics to avoid him, including talking in Hindi between ourselves, but he just wouldn't go. When Gundappa Viswanath entered the group, he greeted the old man with a lot of respect. We knew we had goofed up. Vishy whispered the man's name to us, and we nearly dropped our wine glasses. The old man was Sir Len Hutton, one of the greatest cricketers of all time.

– Anshuman Gaekwad

Roger Codger

Once, Sunil Gavaskar was introducing the team to the then Indian prime minister, Chaudhary Charan Singh. When it was Roger Binny's turn to shake hands with the VIP, the prime minister promptly asked: 'Yeh sahab idhar kyo khade hain. Yeh to foreigner hain.' (Why is this white man standing here? He is a foreigner.) Sunil spent a lot of time explaining to him that Roger was indeed part of the Indian team.

– Sandeep Patil

Yash Talk

Yashpal Sharma once ran into the dressing room during a Test match complaining of a burning sensation. When I asked him what exactly was wrong with him, he said: 'STD ho gaya hai. Yeh mujhe pahle kabhi nahin hua hai.' (I have STD, and this has never happened to me before). It took me a while to recover from the shock, but I could only laugh when I realised that Yash was trying to tell us that he had 'acidity' and that he had never had this problem earlier. The dressing room cracked up in unison.

– Anshuman Gaekwad

Size Unwise

A Mumbai club cricketer (who shall remain unnamed) was touring Australia with his club team. His local host, an Aussie, took him and his colleagues to a mall on an off day. The mall was about to close while our friend was in a shoe shop. 'Hey mate,' said the host, 'why are you taking so long?' 'I can't find my shoe size,' was the reply. The Aussie asked, 'What's your size?' 'Half past nine!' was the reply.

– Hemant Kenkre

Bhajji's Mask-erade

Harbhajan Singh found a nice way of beating boredom on our tour to Sri Lanka in 2002. During one of the non-match evenings, Bhajji wore a dreadful mask and went to every room on his floor. Sourav Ganguly and his wife Dona screamed at the sight, while Rahul Dravid almost dropped dead in fear.

– Virender Sehwag

Prank Frank

Left-arm spinner Dilip Doshi was a favourite victim of our pranks during the 1982 tour of England. Traditionally, the host association keeps bats in the dressing room for each of the players to autograph. On the third day of the Old Trafford Test (in which I hit Bob Willis for six fours in an over), I managed to flick Dilip's bat and kept it among the other bats for autographs. Dilip was livid when he saw his bat decorated with signatures at the end of the day. He then had to go through the ordeal of scratching out all those markings. On the fifth day, I did the same thing. To say Dilip was angry would be an understatement. Off he went to manager Raj Singh Dungarpur with an official complaint of harassment. Needless to say, Rajbhai played the perfect sport and there was no reprimand, much to Dilip's consternation.

– Sandeep Patil

Oil's Well

This may be apocryphal, but a reliable source once told me this hilarious story: A former Indian cricketer of the '70s, best known for his close-in catching, went to a car mechanic. 'I have lost a screw cap in my car bonnet on which was written 710,' he said. 'Can you replace it?' The mechanic had no idea, so he asked his colleagues. They were just as bewildered and asked him to write it down. He carefully wrote 710. It was only because the mechanics looked at the paper upside down that they could understand what he was saying: OIL.

– Kersi Meher-Homji

Cheeka Charlie

On the historic 1982 tour to Pakistan, Jehangir Khan, Sunil Gavaskar, Gundappa Viswanath and Javed Miandad were being felicitated at a Lahore hotel. Our manager, Maharaja Fatehsinghrao Gaekwad, was mindful of protocol – 'No masti (pranks),' we were told. Sunil ventured to ask about Krishnamachari Srikkanth, who, he said, kept making faces while clearing his nose. The Maharaja said: 'Cheeka, don't do it.' Kris found it hard, but he agreed not to clear his nose. 'I won't let my team down,' he committed. But clearing his nose was like breathing for Cheeka, he could not live without doing it. And true to form, he cleared his nose the moment he shook hands with Gen Zia ul-Haq. The entire team was in splits.

– Sandeep Patil

Leg Side

On the tour to Pakistan in 1982, Sandeep Patil seemed to be angry at something *The Times of India* journalist R. Sriman had written. During the series, Sandeep suffered his customary leg injury. When the two met the next time, Sriman asked him how his leg was. 'Hairy,' was Sandeep's one-word reply before walking off in a huff.

– Kuldip Lal

Ray-sing the finger

Ray Jordan, Australia's reserve wicketkeeper on the 1969 tour of India, was definitely not a role model for Adam Gilchrist – he didn't believe in 'walking'. Jordan took an umpire's finger raising as a personal affront. It so happened that in the match against South Zone, Australia were in deep trouble with Jordan and captain Bill Lawry fighting a rear guard action. Just before tea, however, Jordan's vigil came to an abrupt end when he played forward to off-spinner Erapalli Prasanna, giving a bat-pad catch to a close-in fielder.

The umpire raised his finger, and as he was walking back to the pavilion, Jordan asked him: 'How was that out?' 'Mr Jordan, you are out caught,' replied the umpire. 'I couldn't be out caught,' argued Jordan, 'I didn't hit it.' 'Well, if you didn't hit it you are out LBW,' said the implacable umpire. 'Caught or LBW, Mr Jordan, take your pick.'

– Ian Chappell

Kambli Couture

During one of our Cooch Behar Trophy tours, I challenged my friend and teammate Vinod Kambli to wear a skirt. The irrepressible Vinod did not think twice before asking what the reward would be. I told him I would be his slave for life. Within minutes, Vinod was all over the streets of Ahmedabad wearing a skirt. He removed it only when we returned to the hotel at 11 pm.

– Sachin Tendulkar

Zed Zed Zed

During the 2004 India-Pak series, I met Zaheer Abbas thrice in the space of one week, in different cities. 'Zed' is known to enjoy his drink even during the day but I did not smell it on his breath once. He was, however, a little dizzy. Each time I walked up to greet him, he would look at me quizzically, and I would re-introduce myself. It happened at the PIA office, at the cricket ground, and later, at the airport. Each time he would feign recognition and say, 'Of course, of course.' The last time, in Karachi, I just made up a story: 'We met at Yusuf Salli's party,' I told him. And pat came his reply: 'Of course, of course.'

We might remember Zaheer's great batting, but obviously his memory seemed clean bowled.

– Aakar Patel

Frog Ugh

Gundappa Viswanath, Syed Kirmani, B.S. Chandrasekhar and I reached the Windward Islands late one night during our 1975-76 West Indies tour. We entered the first restaurant we laid our eyes on, a place, we found out, that had only 'Mountain Chicken and Rice' – everything else on its menu was over as it was just about closing time.

Famished as we were and left with no choice, we ordered it and, in fact, relished it. The next day, we made sure we headed for dinner early so that we did not miss out on the other sumptuous offerings on the menu. Out of sheer curiosity, we asked the waiter the reason for the dish being called Mountain Chicken. 'Is it because they are found in the mountains?' I asked. 'Yes, maaan, they are,' he replied in a heavy baritone. 'What do they look like?' I persisted. 'They look like frogs, maaan. Actually, they *are* frogs.'

The moment he uttered these words, our appetite suddenly disappeared! We saw only frogs in our mind's eye, and they were certainly not appetising. All of us then had to visit the rest rooms to disgorge our previous night's culinary intakes. And yes, we stayed away from anything remotely associated with chicken for the entire tour.

– Anshuman Gaekwad

Siva Viva

On the eve of the memorable Pakistan tour of 1982-83, we were put up at the Oberoi in Mumbai. Around 7.30 pm, when we hit the room's mini bar, L. Sivaramakrishnan joined us and after a lengthy chat, left. The moment he closed the door, the power tripped. After a while it got a bit stuffy inside, so I opened the door, and whom did I see?

Siva, still standing there. I asked him what he was doing alone in the dark corridor. Siva's reply had us in splits. 'Sandybhai,' he said, 'the corridor is dark, and so am I. If I walk down the corridor, someone would definitely bump into me, and I would surely be slapped.'

– Sandeep Patil

Ball Bail

Our school was certainly not the hottest in Bangalore when it came to cricketing infrastructure. Our passion for the game, however, emboldened us to walk up to the principal and request better facilities. The physical training inspector, who doubled up as a cricket coach, got us a new mat, but when we asked for new balls, there was a frown. He said: 'We have got you a new mat, so why do you need new balls?'

– Rahul Dravid

Hit and Mrs

I was playing with the Dundee Club in the Scottish League in 1985. I was pretty quick then. During one match, I hurled a bouncer that hit the batsman, whose name I cannot recall. He started bleeding.

No sooner had this happened than his wife came running on to the field, gave me a tight slap and said: 'Why are you trying to kill my husband?' She was about to give me another slap when her husband stopped her.

– Raju Kulkarni

Belly Laughs

There was a great Indian player whose vocabulary would never go down well with the Queen, but as long as he made cricket history consistently with his all-round performance, who cared if he also hit the language for a six! One amusing incident, however, would rest the case for the prosecution. On one England tour, the great player in question played a blinder against a county team even as the rest of the batting collapsed. An impressed junior player said as he unbuckled his pads, 'Well played, sir.' The slasher responded: 'You must have belly in the fire to play like that!' Obviously the junior player could not stomach that one.

– Clayton Murzello

Unc Funk

On Day One of the Kanpur Test in the 1973 series between India and England, Sunil Gavaskar was finding his true touch for the first time in the five-Test series. During one Chris Old over, there was a loud appeal for LBW off the last ball, which the umpire negated. During the changeover, all-rounder Tony Greig passed by Sunil and remarked: 'That was close, wasn't it, Sunny?' 'It was,' agreed Sunny, 'the umpire's my uncle!' Word spread in the England team that the umpire was Sunil's uncle – Gothoskar... Gavaskar... the names seemed to come from the same family! Left to Tony Greig, England would have sent in a written protest, objecting to Gavaskar's 'uncle' Gothoskar officiating in a Test match at a time when India was leading 2-1 in the series.

– Raju Bharatan

Menu Vasu!

At the CCI in the 1960s, Bombay were playing a Ranji Trophy match in which Vasu Paranjape was the 12th man. The great Bapu Nadkarni, ever a cranky man, asked Vasu for a cup of tea during a break. At the next halt, he asked him for a banana. On yet another stoppage, he asked Vasu for some biscuits. At the next break, however, Vasu was ready – with the menu card, asking Bapu to select whatever he wanted for the next break so he could keep it ready.

– Sandeep Patil

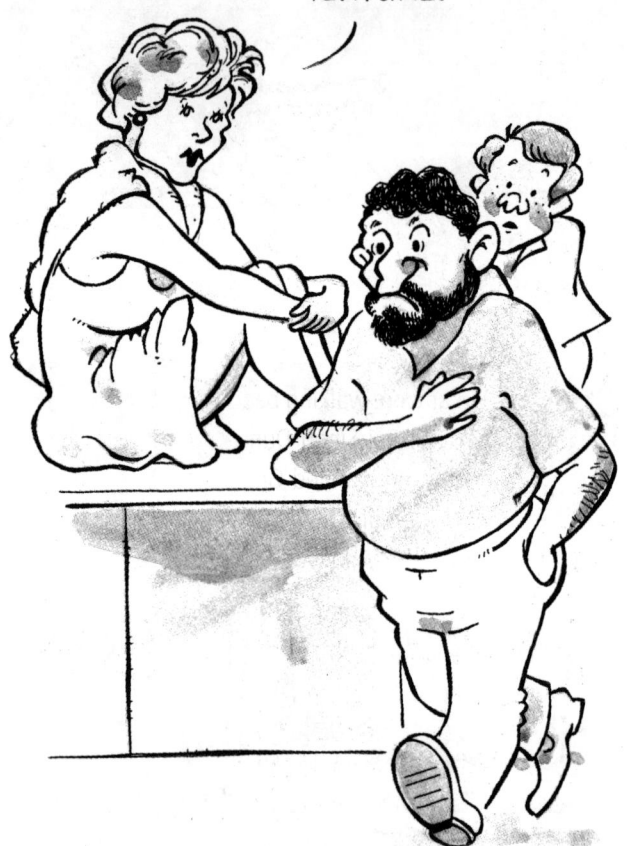

Naïve Mate

Pranab Roy and Ghulam Parkar were walking back to their hotel after an Indian meal on the 1982 England tour. Raj Singh Dungarpur and I were only a few paces ahead of them. Suddenly, Pranab and Ghulam were approached by two extremely good-looking, yet gaudily made-up women who asked them: 'Looking for business?' Ghulam, who was naïve and had not yet been introduced to the busy nightlife in England, said: 'What business? I already have a job. I play for India and the Mafatlal Sports Club.' Pranab nudged and winked at him and said in a loaded tone: 'They are offering you business, don't you understand?' Ghulam did not. Meanwhile, we ran to Ghulam's rescue, and when we explained things to him, his colour turned bright red with embarrassment.

– Sandeep Patil

Bye-the-way, He's Leaving

Ted Dexter's MCC were playing a tour game against Rajasthan during the 1961-62 series. It was a historic game for us as it was the end of the great Vinoo Mankad's illustrious career – his last first-class game. Mankad was in a hurry; he had to reach Bombay for the thread ceremony of his two sons, and needed to leave early to catch a flight at around five in the evening. It didn't help him any that the tourists were playing with confidence. John Murray was well settled and was arrogantly stepping out against our bowlers. As time ticked by, we became increasingly desperate. Just before the tea interval, I decided to play on Mankad's mind a little. Fielding at mid-on, I shouted in his direction, 'Master, tamaro nasto banawe che.' [Master, he (the batsman) is making a meal of you.] Mankad quipped back, 'Arre na, daano nakhoon choo.' (No, I am just feeding him.) In the over that turned out to be the last one he bowled in cricket, Mankad flighted his deliveries well, drawing Murray out of the crease. The last ball was a fast full toss. It flew straight on to the bat and went straight back to Mankad, who accepted it with both hands, threw the ball to me, and said, 'Bye.'

– Raj Singh Dungarpur
(Courtesy: Nagaraj Gollapudi / Wisden Asia Cricket)

Turban Take-Off

On a flight to Delhi with the Mumbai Ranji Trophy team in the mid-1980s, our opening bowler Balwinder Singh Sandhu requested us not to disturb him as he was keen on catching up on some sleep. 'Why should we disturb you, Ballu? Go on and get some sleep,' said Sandeep Patil. While Sandhu dozed, Sandeep revisited his craft skills and made a paper rocket which he then inserted with soft hands in Ballu's turban. Ballu woke up to the smell of a steaming hot meal and noticed the air hostess smiling away at him. Ballu wasn't used to female following, but he probably felt good in the head. The movement of his rocketed head as he tucked into his supper made entertaining viewing and Ballu found fellow passengers smiling at him. When he discovered his 'antenna' there was only one way to look – towards Sandy, who, as usual, pleaded innocence.

– Chandrakant Pandit

Smokin' Joke

Once during an interview, I asked former India great Vijay Manjrekar when he began smoking. The reply came in the blink of an eye: 'When the Indian team was all out for 42 on a perfect batting track at Lord's in 1974.'

– Pradeep Vijayakar

Heart-y Laugh

The Cooch Behar Room at the Cricket Club of India was the venue of a press conference to announce India's tour party to the West Indies in 1997 – a few seasons before Board president Jagmohan Dalmiya decided that the chairman of selectors would not have to be answerable to the media after selection meetings.

This time, however, chairman Ramakant Desai had to go through the ordeal of explaining the committee's decisions. The surprise package of the selection was the inclusion of Navjot Singh Sidhu, who had only recently abandoned the tour of England after a misunderstanding.

Rajan Bala, a senior journalist, got up and asked, 'Tiny (Desai's nickname), why this change of heart on Sidhu?' Poor Desai, already nervous about answering an array of questions, had got a beamer first up. Since I occupied one of the early rows in the hall, I managed to hear what Desai asked Dalmiya (the Board's secretary). 'What is wrong with Sidhu's heart?' Dalmiya then explained that Bala wanted to know why the selectors had decided to include Sidhu. The room did not break into laughter as not many had heard the exchange, but I had difficulty keeping a straight face.

– Clayton Murzello

Miandad on Song

During the Lahore Test in 1989-90, also Javed Miandad's 100th, the Pakistani great was batting in his 90s and should have been concentrating on getting to his century when he broke into a Hindi film song. He went on to score 145. In all my tours, I have never seen a player singing while batting in a Test match, that too while approaching a special landmark (Miandad is only the second batsman, after Gordon Greenidge, to score a century in both his first and 100th Tests). Sanjay Manjrekar was fielding at short-leg, and Javed asked us which song we would like to hear next. It was hilarious, but also incredible.

– Kiran More

(Courtesy: H. Natrajan / Wisden Asia Cricket)

Goyal Gone

I am still looking for a cricketer called Goyal from Rajasthan who took my pads during an under-15 camp. Those pads were special to me since Sunil Gavaskar had presented them to me. Also, I had got pretty used to them by then and I had a match coming up. So Goyal, wherever you are, please give me back my pads!

– Sachin Tendulkar

Sunny Side Up

At Lord's, during the 1982 tour, we had to go through the Grace Gates even for practice. Ravi (Shastri) and I were in cricket clothing with kitbags. Sunil (Gavaskar) had taken the day off and followed us in a jacket. When we reached the gate, I told the attending steward, pointing to Sunil: 'This gentleman, who is following us, is harassing us. He will claim to be the Indian team's captain, but don't believe that rubbish.' Naturally, Sunil had a big argument with the steward. He literally pleaded with him, saying, 'I am Sunil Gavaskar.'

The steward replied nonchalantly: 'Nothing doing, everybody says he is Gavaskar. Where are your cricket clothes?' Sunil replied that he was not wearing any flannels, but that he was indeed India's cricket captain. It was only after some 15 minutes of arguing that we went to Sunil's rescue.

– Sandeep Patil

Picture Imperfect

To say that the Indian and Pakistani media went overboard during India's historic tour to Pakistan in 2004 would be an understatement. Anybody who was somebody was being interviewed, and I was tempted to tell one Indian journalist to interview a few cobblers from Multan's streets!

The Pakistan media were no less active. In Multan, as I was returning from lunch, a Pakistani photographer asked me to pose with former player Intikhab Alam, which I did. I awoke next morning to see the photograph in a leading Urdu paper with a caption that read, 'Bishen Singh Bedi and Intikhab Alam, two stalwarts of Indian and Pakistani cricket.' Did I use the word overboard above? Make that crazy!

– Harpal Singh Bedi

Two Fingers to Him

There was this gentleman who was sent abroad for the first time in his life as a Hindi commentator with Bishan Singh Bedi's team to Australia in the '70s. At the end of Day One in the first Test at Perth, India were in a position of strength. Left-arm spinner Tony Mann was sent out as night watchman, and amazingly, he not only deprived India of an expected win, but went on to steer Australia to victory. The Test had been preceded by a pre-series media campaign alleging that Bhagwat Chandrasekhar — he with the freak bowling arm — was a chucker.

Imagine the scenario of the last morning: India, with their tails up, sniffing victory; Australia fighting for dear life. In the first session Chandra raps Mann on the pads. The umpire negates the confident leg-before appeal. Next ball: action replay. Later, with Australia looking like saving the Test, a repeat of the leg-before appeal. This time, the Indians have no doubt Mann is plumb. 'Not out,' is again the verdict. Chandra snatches his cap from the umpire and walks to his customary fine-leg fielding position to jeers of 'Chandra chucker, Chandra chucker' from the partisan crowd.

This prompts the normally genial, but now agitated, Chandra to give the crowd the famous two-finger Aussie salute. At which stage, the commentator, poor innocent abroad, describes the incident to his listeners back home thus: 'Ab Chandra fielding karne jaa rahe hain. Log chilla rahe hain "Chandra chucker", "Chandra chucker".' ('Chandra is now going to his fielding position, and the crowd is chanting "Chandra chucker", "Chandra chucker".') Raising his two fingers, a la Chandra, our commentator friend explains: 'Aur Chandra unse keh rah hain, "Woh ek bar nahin, do bar out thhé!"' ('And Chandra is explaining to them, "He was out not merely once, but twice!"')

– Khalid A-H Ansari

Coach Nose Best

At a coaching camp for juniors in north India, the coach peppered his lessons with cricket theory and jargon. One wide-eyed boy took his coach's advice a little too seriously. As he was padding up to bat in the nets, his coach came to him and exhorted him to 'smell the ball'. The boy nodded, and made his way to the net. He took his guard and prepared to face the first ball. It turned out to be a short delivery. The coach and everybody else watched as the batsman saw the ball leave the bowler's hand, and watched it all the way, till it hit his… nose! The boy collapsed in a pool of blood, and his coach rushed to him. 'What happened, why didn't you play it with the bat,' the coach asked. 'Sir, you told me to smell the ball, so I went forward to smell it,' the dizzy boy said. It may have amused the people around, but the coach was certainly red!

– Ashok Mankad
(Courtesy: Devendra Prabhudesai)

Ton-in-cheek retort

It was Shane Warne's debut Test at Sydney, where Ravi Shastri was waging two battles – one against Australian bowling, and the other against sledging. During his knock, he took a quick single which the substitute fielder saw as a run-out chance. But when he realised that Shastri would make his ground, he did not throw the ball. Instead, he shrieked: 'Next time, I'll blow your f***ing head off.' Not one to keep quiet, the ever-ready Shastri retorted: 'If your bowling was as good as your throwing, you wouldn't be Australia's 12th man.' Every single Australian fielder cracked up. Shastri then went on to belt Warne and the other bowlers to a historic double hundred in that innings.

– Clayton Murzello

Delivery Dialogue

There was this very promising pace bowler from Maharashtra in the early '70s, who was built like a wrestler but, sadly, displayed all the qualities of a country bumpkin. To prepare him to retaliate against the short stuff aimed at Indian batsmen by the demon bowlers of West Indies, Australia and England, this pace bowler was sent to Alf Gover's Cricket School in England for fine-tuning. As many had expected, he learnt precious little on the trip, but returned after contracting pneumonia and losing his bowling rhythm in the bargain. When his teammates asked him about his stay in England, he said, 'Arre...You'll be surprised! The British kids are not like our kids, you know. Even two- and three-year-olds speak fluent English there!'

– Sandeep Patil

Walk Knock

I was sharing a room with Sachin Tendulkar during his debut tour of Pakistan in 1989-90. One night, I woke up to check whether everything was okay with my young roomie. To my horror, the sixteen-year-old was not in bed. I searched everywhere in the hotel – the lobby, the toilets, the corridors, but our guy was not to be found. Something told me to take one final look on the terrace. And there he was – sleepwalking!

– Kiran More

Blow Hot, Blow Cold

During our England tour of 1979, we played Gloucestershire, then a formidable side with players like Mike Proctor, Zaheer Abbas and Sadiq Mohammed. Skipper Venkataraghavan asked me to open the bowling, and I responded by taking 5 for 75 after 21 overs on the trot.

However, their tail wagged, and they finally went on to beat us, by getting us out cheaply in the second innings. The long spell, though, told on my legs. I decided to soak luxuriously in a hot bath, having done what I presumed was a good day's work. Venkat, on the other hand, had other ideas. He decided I should bat at No 3. I grumbled, but to no effect. Proctor bowled the most lethal inswingers and had me groping at the first three deliveries. I went up to the umpire as a last resort to complain about the light and the sightscreen. My complaints fell on deaf ears, and a low inswinger did me in. Humiliated and bruised, I was even shown the direction to the pavilion lest I could not see it. The dressing room sniggers were no better. Finding the captain near the tub, I called out, 'Skip, can you just check whether the water is still hot for a bath?' If looks could kill, I would have been dead meat then, but the atmosphere relaxed when the team burst out laughing.

– Yajurvindra Singh

Question Time

Sanjay Manjrekar would go to any length to learn more about the game. At the Worli office of Nirlon, a team that had some of India's best players on its rolls, Manjrekar sought an appointment with Sunil Gavaskar. He spoke for a couple of minutes before asking a nervous question, 'Sir, when you faced the fast bowlers from the West Indies, did you ever see the ball?'

Sunil had scored 13 of his 34 Test centuries against them!

– Mudar Patherya

Literal Laughs

When Sandeep Patil returned from his first trip to England, he did not forget to buy a good St Peter's cricket shirt for his coach. A few days later, when the hard-hitter visited the nets to meet his coach, he was surprised that the coach's shirt was wet and dripping. 'What's wrong, sir? Why is your shirt wet?' inquired Sandeep. 'Don't tell me you don't know, Sandeep!' replied the coach, knowingly. 'The shirt says – "Wash and Wear!"'

– Clayton Murzello

Trupen-dously Funny

Abdul Ismail, one of Mumbai's most talented fast bowlers never to have played for India (he claimed 198 wickets in the Ranji Trophy), invariably had a short-leg fielder. In a local club match, a batsman got an inner edge to an Abdul delivery with the ball lodging into his pads, thus rendering the ball 'dead'. A subdued appeal later, as we were walking back to our positions, we saw the short-leg fielder Trupen Desai running circles around the batsman in the hope that the ball would fall down and he could catch it. Every single player cracked up at this spectacle, and we never let Trupen forget his strange lack of understanding of basic cricket rules. Funnily enough, Trupen went on to become an umpire after he retired from local cricket!

– Bharat Kunderan

Holland Howler

For many years, I managed Sunder Cricket Club, which had players who went on to play for Mumbai in the Ranji Trophy, and even for India. One cricketer, who was on assignment to play club cricket in England, decided to visit the Netherlands for a brief post-season holiday. This cricketer had a great sense of humour, despite being ill at ease with the English language. But he was quite sporting about it, too. On his arrival in Holland, a customs officer asked him: 'Do you have a CD player?' Flummoxed, the young man replied: 'Not at all, I am a cricket player.' He was obviously inspired by Oscar Wilde who once said: 'I have nothing to declare except my genius.'

– Clayton Murzello

Teller Trapped

I had gone to Mahabaleshwar (a hill station near Mumbai) for a short holiday and noticed a fortune-teller near our hotel. One morning I decided to ask him what was in store for me. To my utter surprise, he could tell me all about my cricket career, such as how I moved from Saurashtra to Mumbai to make a mark in first-class cricket. I offered to pay another Rs 100 if he could tell me how he was able to gather all this information. The fortune-teller fell for it and revealed that Sandeep Patil, who was in Mahabaleshwar the previous week, had told him all about me!

– Karsan Ghavri

All Balls

Abdul Jabbar was doing 12th man duties for South Zone against West Zone in Baroda in 1976 and was needed on the field when the ball went out of shape. The commentator chose to describe the scene thus: 'Jabbar is running with his balls because the umpire's balls have lost shape.'

– Makarand Waingankar

Durrani's Sweet 16

It must have been the second Ranji match of my career. I was with Delhi then, and we were playing Rajasthan, which had Salim Durrani, now almost at the end of his career. I had scored a century, and was all charged up for my double. The next day, Durrani bowled down the leg a lot to me, and then turned one sharply to hit my off-stump bail. Being young and excitable, I was quite peeved about that.

Later in the game, Durrani came out to bat. Rakesh Shukla was bowling and I was at slip. I started ribbing Durrani, shouting, 'Come on Rocky, this guy's nervous, let's get him.' Durrani only looked at me. The first ball, he sliced to third man, but softly enough for me to chase it all the way to the fence. The next ball was a rank full toss, but Durrani again sliced it to third man, and again I gave it a long chase. The third ball pitched outside leg, but believe it or not – he withdrew outside the line and sliced it once more to third man. The next ball, you can guess by now, was again hit in that direction for me to run to the fence and fetch it. He had just got four consecutive boundaries. At the end of the over I passed Durrani, huffing and puffing and panting, when he looked at me and said, 'Hum ko bhi thoda cricket aata hai' (Even I know a little bit of cricket.) He was a genius.

– Arun Lal
(Courtesy: Rahul Bhattacharya / Wisden Asia Cricket)

Secy-urity Breach

Mansur Ali Khan, the Nawab of Pataudi, had just been named the captain of the Indian team. He came down to Hyderabad to practice before going to Madras to lead the side. When he entered the ground he saw M.L. Jaisimha facing the bowling of Hyderabad Cricket Association joint secretary Ganesan and other Hyderabad bowlers. Jaisimha was hitting Ganesan all over the field, sending some of the balls on to the roof of the Lal Bahadur Stadium. When Tiger Pataudi padded up and came to bat, the first ball he faced was from Ganesan. It appeared to be a leg break, pitching at least one foot away from the off-stump. Pataudi advanced a little and lifted his bat, not offering a stroke. But to his utter surprise, it was a googly. The ball turned into the stumps, sending the middle stump crashing. Everyone, including Pataudi, burst out laughing! The secretary had got the skipper!

– G. Rajaraman

Taking Guard

While playing against India at Bombay in 1958-59, West Indian great Gary Sobers was caught and bowled by the relatively unknown Ghulam Guard, who was also a policeman by profession. Sobers then remarked: 'This is the most famous arrest he will ever make.' Indeed, Sobers got a hundred in the next Test, and was never dismissed again by the cop.

– Ramachandra Guha

Smoking Break

On a warm summer day at the Rose Bowl in Southampton, the Indians were up against a relatively inexperienced Hampshire team, but the pace of the game was frenzied. The pitch was deteriorating fast, and at one point the Indians threatened to forfeit their second innings. Fortunately, good sense prevailed, and the game went on, but it was largely agreed that none of the frontline fast bowlers would bat long enough to invite injury.

Not everyone in the Hampshire team was entirely happy with this agreement, and it showed when it came to their second innings. Neil Johnson, the former Zimbabwe cricketer, was padded up and ready to go in to bat. Perhaps nervous about batting on the Rose Bowl pitch, he lit a cigarette and puffed away outside the dressing room. When it was time for him to go in, he passed the cigarette on. 'Don't put it out just yet. I don't know how long it will be before I'm back,' he said as he strode out. In the event, Johnson was caught in the slips for a speedy duck and was back in time to claim his cigarette and pick up where he left off! Evidently there was no fire in Johnson's performance, but there was smoke.

– Anand Vasu

Dicky Gets Tricky

'Dicky' Rutnagur was an unstoppable prankster. In the '80s, during an Indian team's tour to Australia, he played a prank on Hindi commentator Jasdev Singh at a Melbourne hotel.

For four successive nights, Dicky filled out the room service breakfast card, from top to bottom, asking for a huge variety of juices, cereals, eggs, savouries, ham, bacon, sausage, an assortment of bread and toast, tea, coffee, the works, and hung it outside Jasdev's room after he had retired for the night. For four consecutive days, Jasdev complained: 'Khalid, pata nahin yeh hotel ki room service kaisi hai. Woh roz mujhe subah savere chaar baje utha dete hain, sab qism ka ajeeb non-veg nashta la kar. Tum to jaante ho main strict vegetarian hoon.' (Khalid, this hotel's room service is rather strange. They wake me up at four every morning with a strange kind of non-vegetarian breakfast. You know I am a strict vegetarian.)

You can be sure Jasdev Singh wasn't amused in the least when he discovered he had been at the receiving end of Dicky's puckish humour.

– Khalid A-H Ansari

Rajbhai Gets Nayudu-Nostalgic

It is difficult to stop Raj Singh Dungarpur when he talks about C.K. Nayudu. At a function to felicitate Rahul Dravid at the MIG Club in Mumbai, Dungarpur regaled the audience with stories that reflected Nayudu's brilliance. Towards the end of his speech, he turned to Rahul Dravid and said, 'You guys (referring to Dravid's generation of players) are lucky. You wouldn't have got any endorsements if C.K. was around.' Only Dungarpur's charm could make him get away with that.

– Clayton Murzello

Lala Gala

The year 1997 was India's fiftieth anniversary of Independence; it was time for nostalgia, to remember heroes of the days gone by. As part of a special series, I had interviewed Lala Amarnath at the NDTV studios. Later, I accompanied him to the *Statesman* office where senior journalist K.N. Mohlajee asked him who he thought were the best players of all time. The veteran cricketer was stuck at only one point – whether to vote for Vinoo Mankad or Bishen Singh Bedi as the country's best left-arm spinner. Eventually he said: 'I would choose Bishen, because he was a master of flight.' He then turned to me with a twinkle in his eye, and whispered: 'And I say that even though I hate that bastard.'

– Gulu Ezekiel

The Wrong 'Un

V. M. Muddiah, who played Test cricket with the great leg spinner Subhash Gupte, remembered fielding in the leg trap on India's 1959 tour of England. At leg slip, Muddiah watched Gupte's hand so as to be able to tell his leg spinner from his googly.

'Forget it,' said teammate Bapu Nadkarni, fielding next to him at short square leg. 'Just watch the batsman, I play with Gupte for Bombay and still cannot read him!'

– Ramachandra Guha

Hine Sight

On his way to England (or maybe on his way back), Sir Don Bradman's ship had docked for a brief while in Colombo, Sri Lanka (then Ceylon). Bradman agreed to play a quick match with a local team. When he was batting, he took a few singles to the best fielder in the Ceylonese side, Rusell Hine. But right in the middle of the innings, Bradman requested the pitch to be measured. And sure enough it was three feet short. When asked how he knew the pitch was short, he replied: 'I took singles to your best fielder, and if this pitch was of normal length, I should have been stretching while taking those singles.'

– Tom Alter

Jamun Jammin'

Once, in the late '80s, Tamil Nadu and my side Karnataka were involved in a thrill-a-minute Ranji Trophy match. We had one problem though. Our ace spinner Raghuram Bhat was down with a sore toe, so much so that each time it touched his shoe, he winced in pain. Several trips to the dressing room later, one senior player had a sudden brainwave – he shoved gulab jamuns left over from lunch into Raghuram's socks to give him the required padding, and it worked!

– Rahul Dravid

Such A 'Fine' Garment

The historic 1980-81 tour of Australia was also one of the most hectic. We were travelling from one venue to the other at a frantic pace; naturally, the team members kept forgetting their things at the hotels. When this became an epidemic of sorts, team manager Wing Commander Durrani and captain Sunil Gavaskar introduced a stiff Aus$50 fine for anybody who left their things behind.

As luck would have it, during a team meeting, we received a sealed bag, with a label indicating that the item inside was left behind at the previous venue. It turned out to be a 'lungi'. There were only two men in the team who wore lungis – batsman Gundappa Viswanath and off-spinner Shivlal Yadav, both south Indians.

It was Durrani who declared Shiv out. He insisted the lungi belonged to Shiv, claiming he had seen him wearing it. Shiv was saving up every dollar to build a house in Hyderabad, and pleaded with the manager not to fine him. But Durrani, armyman that he was, insisted on the disciplinary action, and Shiv had no option but to pay up.

Even today, Shiv denies the lungi was his. Nevertheless, the episode proved what a 'fine' garment the lungi was!

– Sandeep Patil

Pyjama Cricket!

Former Indian Test skipper Nari Contractor once told us this story about Mansur Ali Khan Pataudi's ghost mask. Nari remembered how Tiger Pataudi, a past master in the art of practical jokes, acquired this frightful mask at Port of Spain, Trinidad.

After dinner one evening, Pataudi, Nari, team manager Ghulam Ahmed, and perhaps M.L. Jaisimha or Dicky Rutnagur (he is not sure who) decided to visit K.N. Prabhu, then the sports editor of the *Times of India*, who was touring with the team and staying at the Queen's Park Hotel across the road. Tiger wore the mask and donned a white sheet around him as they crossed the road to the hotel. A passing motorist saw the apparition, screeched his car to a halt and fled for his life.

The group entered the hotel, roaring with laughter at the poor motorist's plight. Ghulam (may his soul rest in peace) was in hysterics, and was so consumed with laughter that he failed to see the swimming pool in the compound in the dark and found himself in the water – suit and all! The pranksters then made their way to Prabhu's room. The venerable TOI correspondent, dressed in his pyjamas, was reading a book. He answered the knock at the door only to run smack into 'Tiger' who, mask, sheet and all, let out an eerie shriek. Prabhu, whose pyjama cord was rather loose, recoiled in horror and fled to the back of the room exclaiming 'Hoo, hoo, hoo,' even as he tried desperately to prevent his pyjamas from falling off!

– Khalid A-H Ansari

Off the Mark

Off days spare no one, as I realised when the England team had a 'Meet the Press' session at the Taj hotel before their tour kicked off in 2001. After I finished a lengthy interview with England batsman Mark Ramprakash, I dashed off to the next table to interview Ashley Giles, armed with a set of questions prepared the night before. England had achieved back-to-back series wins in Sri Lanka and Pakistan before they set foot on Indian shores, so I was keen to know how Giles had found the spin-oriented pitches there. Since it was an open session I noticed that some fellow mediamen were asking batting-related questions. Soon, I realised we were interviewing Marcus Trescothick! I had mistaken him for Giles. I laugh about it now, but I burned with shame that day.

– Clayton Murzello

Service with a Salaam

Despite their problems with food and accommodation, the 1969-70 Australian team to India encountered genuine hospitality. Ashley Mallett writes in *Spin Out* (Gary Sparke and Associates): 'The bearers were delightful little people. They were all smiles, but for some reason we were a trifle suspicious of them. I gained the habit of saluting them. Each one I saw I would command to salute with: "Salaam, sir!" They returned the salute with a like retort. Other players found the bearers saluting them and I was blamed for this inconvenience.'

– Ashley Mallett

Marshalling the Courage to Face Malcolm

It was not without reason that Malcolm Marshall was one of the most dreaded bowlers of all time. In 1978, when Marshall first came to India, he announced his intentions by flooring West Zone batsman Stanley Saldanha with a fierce bouncer. A pool of blood welcomed me to the batting crease. Marshall walked up to me and said: 'Maan, I am going to do the same to you.'

Somehow, instead of instilling fear in me, his remark riled me, and I hit the first delivery through midwicket for four. I walked up to him and retorted, 'I hit slow bowlers square, I guess you need to bowl faster.' Well, he did bowl faster, but on a docile Baroda track, Marshall did not threaten at all. A year later, India were playing Hampshire, and I walked in to join Sunil Gavaskar, who had scored a century. At the end of the over, Sunil asked, 'Do you have a problem with Marshall, as he has specifically requested the captain to bowl a spell to you.' I narrated the Baroda incident to him after Marshall had rained a few bouncers on me, hoping to get some sympathy. Instead, Sunil just laughed. Marshall's next bouncer was dispatched to the hospitality tent for a six. This angered him, and he tried harder to knock me down, but during one delivery he pulled his hamstring muscle and had to be carried off the field.

Later that day, I went up to the dressing room, and said: 'Malcolm maan, I tried sending you a clear message to go to the hospitality tent to have a drink. Now only if you had taken it seriously.' I felt good getting the better of him, but was hoping that I would never ever have to encounter him again in my life. The next time we met was when West Indies came to India in the early 1980s, when

I had just announced my retirement. Malcolm met me at the welcoming dinner at Bombay Gymkhana and said, 'Vindra, when are we playing against each other?' 'I have retired,' I told him. 'You cannot,' he shot back, 'we need to settle scores.' The conversation, however, ended with a friendly drink, but in the middle of it all, he asked, 'When am I playing Dilip Vengsarkar?' I sent a fervent prayer for Dilip that night. The lion was still on the prowl for his next victim.

– Yajurvindra Singh

Words Come Easy, Catches Don't

Cricket writers the world over do not hesitate to carp at and criticise players' techniques and performances. However, cricketers would have had a field day describing a journalists' match at Chembur in Mumbai.

As one batsman lofted the ball in the air, the long-on and long-off fielders ran towards the ball, but neither was keen on taking the catch. The usual shout of 'Mine' was replaced by 'Yours! Yours!' and the catch was expectedly dropped. Moral of the story? People in glass houses should not throw the proverbial stone.

– S.S. Ramaswamy

Kite Caper

This is not just my favourite story, but Sachin Tendulkar's too. During a school match we were playing against Morarji, I was on strike, on 127, and Sachin was on 157, when a kite flew by me. The bowler had already started his run-up, and was about to deliver when I stopped him. I grabbed the dangling string of the kite and began flying it. Everybody was just amazed at first; eventually the entire team started laughing. Later, when we gathered for the post-match analysis with Ramakant Achrekar Sir, we were going through the motions when he paused to bring up one point: 'Vinod Kambli, flying a kite.' He was furious and slapped me so hard I began crying. At the back, I could see Sachin laughing away. He still calls it the funniest moment of his life.

– Vinod Kambli

(Courtesy: Rahul Bhattacharya / Wisden Asia Cricket)

Utter-ly Stutter-ly Hilarious

One of Mumbai's best cricketers captained his side at both the school and college levels. He was famous for two things – his obvious ability as a cricketer, and his 'stammering'. But he was (and is) an optimist, who believed in making the most of whatever he had, or rather, didn't have! He put his 'drawback' to good use at an inter-collegiate match. His counterpart tossed the coin, and as it went up in the air, our stammerer went 'Aaaaaa', unable to complete what he had started. The coin descended to earth, hit the ground and rolled, but our hero still hadn't expressed himself. Finally, the coin became stationary, and guess what our man did? He saw the side on which the coin had fallen (Heads), turned to his counterpart and said, 'Heads, I win! Will bat!' and walked off! Now it was his counterpart's turn to be at a loss for words.

– Ashok Mankad
(Courtesy: Devendra Prabhudesai)

Kandli Bear With Me

Harendra Upadhaya, with whom I played at Khar Gymkhana, was quite a character. He was also a very sound batsman who would have probably played a higher level of cricket if not for this story, which I heard in my formative years. When Harendra was in college, he used to often go to the sports officer armed with applications for cricket equipment. His notes were like this. 'Dear Sir, Kandli provide a new bat for the season; Kandli arrange for a box of balls.' Soon, Harendra acquired the nickname Kandli. Years later, since he got a lot of runs, Ramakant Desai, the India fast bowler, asked him to apply for a job with the Associated Cement Companies, Desai's employers. When Tiny (Desai's nickname) met Harendra the next time, he admonished him for not applying as he had not seen his name on the list. Indeed, Harendra had applied, but Desai was looking out for the name Kandli!

– Bharat Kunderan

Saab-ash Naga!

In India, we did meet some real characters. Naga was one. He was a bearer in Hyderabad. He served in our dining room and never seemed to stop smiling. I remember Bob Cunis having him on. 'Naga, my good man, we never seem to get the best part of the bird, do we? Are you sure we have the best pieces out here?' 'Oh yes, saab. Oh yes,' said Naga. 'Surely this thing here looks like a crow,' Cunis carried on. 'Oh no, no, it is definitely chicken, saab.' He kept repeating the phrases, 'I get for you saab, I get for you.' And 'don't mention it, don't mention it.'

Bob said to him once. 'Look, Naga, if we thank you for something there is no need for you to say "don't mention it".' 'Don't mention it, saab, don't mention it,' said Naga instantly. 'Look Naga, don't say that because we mean thank you when we say thank you. There is no need for you to say "don't mention it,"' said one of us. 'Don't mention it,' repeated Naga for the hundredth time. At that point we thought we had better accept it.

On another occasion, one of the boys was banging the salt out of the shaker because of the humidity in the air. While it was being banged on the table, we suddenly heard a shout from the kitchen. 'I get for you, saab, I get for you.'

– Glenn Turner in
My Way (Hodder and Stoughton)

Forest Fables

Things couldn't have been more important for me in my first Irani Trophy match in Nagpur in 1984-85. A good performance here could get me into the Indian team. The evening before the match, Sandeep Patil suggested we go to the forest nearby. 'We will return by 10.30 pm latest,' he assured me. After all, we were to play the next day. As a young player it was difficult to decline an invitation from a senior player for an adventure. But, thanks to Sandeep's love for the jungle, we came back only at 1.30 am. After somehow managing to get ready on time we met Chandu Borde, who was there to watch the match as chairman of selectors. 'Big day today for you, Chandu,' my namesake told me. 'Keep well, keep well.' Sandeep, standing beside me, remarked: 'Sir, how will he keep well? He returned to his hotel room only at 1.30 this morning.' Now, that was cruel, I thought. But I had to defend myself. 'No sir, Sandeep is bluffing,' I pleaded with him. I don't know whom the chairman believed, but I got picked.

— Chandrakant Pandit

Sachin-teresting Lore

Sachin was among my trainees at the national camp in Indore in 1987. I was reminded of his obsession for practice one night with a knock on the door. It was the watchman complaining that a boy from the camp was keeping everybody awake with the sound of the willow hitting leather behind a closed door. 'Which boy,' I asked the watchman after the rude awakening. 'Woh chhota gora chhokra' (that small, fair boy), he said. I took no time to figure out that it was Sachin. I did not know what to tell the watchman except 'What are you doing here? Go and field for him!'

– Vasu Paranjape

Tribal-ulations

When I got married to Mohini in 1987, there was no time to go on a honeymoon. The very next day after the wedding, I was to go for a Ranji game to Valsad. That evening, my teammates said they would have a small party for me at the hotel. Expecting a wholesome reception, I walked into the room and was surprised to see not a soul, but loud music. Then suddenly a bunch of 'tribals' emerged from somewhere and surprised us both. It happened to be my teammates, some of whom my bride did not know well. Sulakshan Kulkarni led the pack with his jumping down from somewhere, which frightened my wife no end. It took a while before we recognised them all. It was an unforgettable wedding night, all right!

– Chandrakant Pandit

Buch Ado About the Lion

In 1989, as part of the Brijesh Patel Cricket Clinic Team, we visited the Amboselli National Park in Kenya. Our vehicle had veterans such as Brijesh and Roger Binny, apart from juniors. A second vehicle with others from the team got stuck on a damp patch. This prompted drivers of both vehicles to exhort all the team members to get out of the bus and push the stuck vehicle out of the patch. Now we had just been shown a gruesome video by our host Atul Patel about how a Japanese tourist was eaten alive by a pride of lions when he made the mistake of getting out of his vehicle. However, we reluctantly got out. Just then, one of us spotted a huge lion. The drivers immediately yelled at us to get back into the respective vans. We ran faster than we ever ran between the wickets, got back inside, and locked the doors. All, that is, except one. Roger saw one of the Under-13 lads near the rocks, attending to nature's call. He yelled out, prompting the lad, who went by the name of Valmik Buch, to sprint back in. Buch went on to play for Karnataka and Baroda, but never forgot the roaring time we had at the safari.

– Satish Viswanathan

Redders Sees Red

Ian Redpath, a keen fisherman, took time off in Kanpur to fish in the stream near the Kamala Retreat. A placid soul, Ian was sitting on the banks with a couple of his teammates, dangling his line in the water, when a group of Indians spotted them. They caused a great commotion and their waving and yelling almost certainly scared away any fish in the area. This was too much for Redders. He picked up a large piece of wood and, in the best traditions of the Great White Hunter, charged at the startled Indians. He may not have done much for Indo-Australian relations but at least he was left in peace for the rest of the day and managed to catch a few fish.

– Ashley Mallett

Beedi-ng a Hasty Retreat

In the early '70s, the Mumbai team travelled to Bulsad (now Valsad) to play their Ranji Trophy fixture against Gujarat. On match eve, the team was invited for a party hosted by Muthuseth, owner of the famous P.V.S. Beedi Company. As usual, the team had a good time. When it came to saying goodbye, the host presented captain Ajit Wadekar with a video camera. Ajit was very proud of his possession... until the next morning. After the toss, the friendly host took Ajit aside and asked him if he could endorse his product and be available for a quick commercial shoot. Ajit was bewildered, but politely turned down the request. He even returned the video camera, thus proving that nothing in life comes free, especially video cameras!

– Milind Rege

Chatfield Charge

Bangalore, always a favourite destination for touring cricket teams, was not so for New Zealand in 1988-89 when four of their top players came down with the infamous Delhi Belly, forcing the Kiwis to call upon former captain Jeremy Coney, who was then commentating, to help them out on the field along with another commentator. Fast bowler Ewan Chatfield, one of the affected players, ran into bowl from the far end, and kept running past the umpire, the flabbergasted batsman and the equally surprised wicketkeeper, all the way to the dressing room. He re-emerged 15 minutes later wearing a fresh pair of flannels!

– Kuldip Lal

Go Sunny

During the 1982 Faisalabad Test, Sunil Gavaskar was in his 90s when I got up from my seat in the pavilion to go to the toilet. Our manager Fatehsinghrao Gaekwad asked me to hold on until Sunil got his hundred and said that he would give him his watch if he reached the landmark. Usually, no teammate leaves his seat in the dressing room when someone is nearing his century. Though I was desperate to go to the rest room, I obeyed my manager, and sat there. Sunil took nearly one hour to go from 92 to 100; and twenty-five minutes to go from 97 to 100. Naturally, I was cursing. When Sunil finally reached his hundred, the deed was already done – in my pants!

– Sandeep Patil

Toss ka Boss

This one comes from the vast unknown of the Ranji Trophy, circa 1996. The venue was Pune's Nehru Stadium and its famous heartbreaker of a wicket, which was to host the Maharashtra vs Punjab Super League game. No matter what the tinge of green on the wicket or how much grey in the sky above, batting first was the only option for captains winning the toss. The team would bat first, bat once, bat big and shut the opposition out of the match and inevitably take first innings points.

When the Punjab captain returned to the dressing room after the toss he had a big smile on his face. It was like he had been given the keys to the kingdom. The unbelievable had happened – Punjab had won the toss... and opted to field! There were loud whoops in the dressing room and Maharashtra's batsmen set about the Punjab bowling with customary greed. When one of the Maharashtra players bumped into a buddy from the Punjab side during a break, he clapped him on his shoulder and asked why the visitors had chosen to give the home team bowlers such a compliment by not playing them on a first day track. Not that they didn't appreciate the lottery ticket anyway.

The reply from the Punjab man baffled him, 'What lottery ticket? Our captain told us we had lost the toss and Maharashtra had opted to bat!'

– Sharda Ugra

Lala, Kya Maara

Veteran journalist Ragunath Rau paid handsome tributes to Lala Amarnath when the Indian cricket great passed away. He wrote: 'Till the end, though, the acidulous comments remained, even if he knew time was at hand. A magazine reporter had the temerity to call up Lala when he was bedridden and ask for an interview. In his typical earthy Punjabi, Lala replied: "I am dying and you want an interview!" One can leave it to the reader's imagination to guess the language that Lala used. We heard another story about how Lala dealt with a persistent journo who kept pestering him for a story. When it got unbearable, Lala called the relentless writer to his room. As soon as he opened the door, he struck him on the face and said, "Now you've got your story! Go and write it."'

– Clayton Murzello

Slip between the Lip

During a women's Test match between India and New Zealand in the 1970s, a Marathi commentator was given his chance to excel in English commentary. During the course of the match in Pune, the New Zealand batswomen started to attack the Indian bowling and so the Indian captain, Shanta Rangaswamy, decided to spread the field. Rangaswamy's first move was thus described: 'Shanta Rangaswamy removes the first slip.' A little bit later, he added, 'Now she has removed the second slip. Now let us see what else she will remove.'

– Makarand Waingankar

Reckless Sachin Gets a 'Life'

At a felicitation function hosted by the Mumbai Cricket Association in 2002, Sachin Tendulkar reeled out names of people he owed a great deal to. He was half way to his seat when he remembered that he had forgotten to thank his wife Anjali. Walking up to the stage again, he said: 'I feel ashamed to have omitted my wife's name and have come back to thank her because I'd like to go back home today!'

– Clayton Murzello

Ump Stump

After marking his run-up, Suryakant More, the former Mumbai University bowler, was asked by the umpire how he was going to bowl so that he could let the batsman know. The umpire expected to hear left-arm over or right-arm over, as is the normal practice. But More declared: 'I am going to bowl very, very fast.'

– Kiran Ashar

The O and Nil Effect

In the '60s there were a lot of reciprocal tours for Mumbai and Pune teams. Not always was one aware of the opposition's strengths. Once, a senior Pune player decided to indulge in some pre-match hype. 'This man will be a danger man for your team. He is our O'Neill (Australia's batting stalwart of the 1950s and 1960s),' he said.

The much-hyped batsman bagged a pair in the match, which gave me an opportunity to have a go at the senior pro. 'Is he your O'Neill because he got an O and Nil in this match?' I asked before the dressing room cracked up.

– Vasu Paranjape

Boundary Dispute

On the historic 1971 tour of England, renowned commentator Brian Johnston was interviewing the batsmen after they were out. He was quite friendly with me throughout the tour and we used to discuss cricket a lot. When I got out he started asking me the questions on the boundary itself and I decided to pull his leg by saying: 'No English.' He kept on asking questions and I kept repeating the same answer until finally in exasperation he said: 'Ajit, you have been talking to me throughout this tour in English. How could you forget English so soon?' To Brian's dismay, I replied: 'Only Hindi.'

– Ajit Wadekar

Waugh-Some

Even during the sunset of his illustrious cricketing career, Steve Waugh was considered the sledger among sledgers. Who would forget his 'You just dropped the World Cup, son' to Herschelle Gibbs in the famous semi-final at the 1999 World Cup in England! Yet, there were times when Waugh was at the receiving end. Like in the 2003-04 series against India Down Under when Waugh was not at his best. It was a series where the Indians had decided to give it back to the Australians, and give it good. How else could one explain the Indian team manager Shivlal Yadav telling Waugh, when he saw him playing cricket with his son: 'Steve, even your son bats better than you.' The Indian team could only say 'Wa(ug)h! Wa(ug)h!' to that one.

– Clayton Murzello

Lala's Two Cents

On an Indian team tour to Pakistan in the '80s, former Indian captain Lala Amarnath was the Press Trust of India (PTI) correspondent. He sent his dispatch to Delhi after the day's play and left the telex room. I was next door recording my piece for the BBC when the telex operator rushed in looking for Lala. He said he had a message from PTI for him. Suddenly, the great man appeared and the note was handed over to him.

The message read: 'Lalaji, you have sent only two paragraphs. Please send all the details of the day's play.' Lala looked at me and at the telex operator and fumed, 'These chaps at the desk do not know the game and they want me to write more. I have written everything in two paragraphs.' Then, he shouted to the operator: 'Look here, you send three or four more paragraphs for me. You know the game, don't you?'

The poor operator showed ignorance of the game and said, 'Lala Saheb, I don't know much, but if you dictate to me I will add to what you have already sent.' 'Ok then,' said Lala, 'let the PTI chaps be happy.' He sat beside the operator and dictated copy that went on and on until the operator said: 'Abhee Sir ye bahut hai!' (Sir, this is enough now!)

– Qamar Ahmed

Ball Call

I was once invited to lend a helping hand at a camp conducted by Bishan Singh Bedi. Bishan dished out a tough assignment to a stout boy – keeping him running for thirty minutes. Once that was done, he was asked to pad up. He was bowled off the first ball. Ball No 2 had the same effect, and so did the third ball. 'Can't you see the ball,' Bishan yelled. 'Sir, with so much of running, I cannot see anything, forget the ball.'

– T.A. Sekhar

Bawa ki Kamaal

The India vs Australia Test at Brabourne Stadium in October 1964 was one of the most exciting I saw. Skipper Mansur Ali Khan Pataudi scored 86 and 53 and Bhagwat Chandrasekhar took eight wickets but the real contributor to this thrilling win was a Parsee bawaji. He was mad about cricket but cricketers avoided him because he brought them bad luck.

To be wished good luck by him meant scoring a duck, dropping a catch or breaking a leg. An enterprising member of the CCI saw a possibility in him. He invited the jinxing bawaji as his guest on the first day of that Test and introduced him to Norm O'Neill. That did it! Ten minutes after the Test started, O'Neill fell ill with a stomach infection and took no part in the Test. His absence was keenly felt as India won by two wickets. Forget Pataudi and Chandra, the bawaji was the real Man of the Match!

– Kersi Meher-Homji

Baig's Cheeky Show

During a Test match in Bombay in 1960, Abbas Ali Baig was kissed by a spectator. 'Where were the girls when I was batting?' Merchant asked, to which A. F. S. Talyarkhan replied: 'Fast asleep!'

– Clayton Murzello

Lights Out for the Night-watchman

Virender Sehwag's dismissal at the fag end of the second day's play at Lord's in 2002 meant that the Indians needed to send in a nightwatchman.

Ashish Nehra, the most inept of the Indian tail, volunteered to do the dirty work and to everyone's surprise, set off. It opened up a scenario where the not-out batsman (Rahul Dravid) needed to protect the nightwatchman more than the other way round.

Nehra got hit on the pads repeatedly and survived a close leg before shout. In the last over of the day, he edged one to third man. Dravid set off for a run but Nehra would not move. Traffic policeman-like, he put up a hand and refused. Dravid ducked his head under his helmet to prevent the cameras from catching his reaction: he was either laughing or cursing.

Two balls later, all fears were realised as Andrew Flintoff hit Nehra on the pad again, and umpire Rudi Koertzen sent the nightwatchman off. And that was good night for Mr Nehra.

– Sharda Ugra

Seven, No Heaven for Raj

A few years ago, cricket enthusiast Chhatrapalsinh Jadeja organised a reunion of Mumbai Ranji Trophy players. It was one of the most enjoyable evenings in Mumbai cricket held at the C.K. Nayudu Banquet Hall of the Cricket Club of India. But conspicuous by his absence was the club's president, Raj Singh Dungarpur.

How could a person like Dungarpur miss a function like that? When I bumped into him the next day, I asked him the all-important question. 'After ending up on the losing side in seven Ranji Trophy finals against those players, I didn't want to open old wounds for myself.' So much for honesty.

– Clayton Murzello